A LONG TIME AGO, WHEN I WAS IN ELEMENTARY SCHOOL, AN OLD MAN WOULD COME AROUND MY NEIGHBORHOOD TO PERFORM A *KAMI-SHIBAI* ("PAPER PLAY") SHOW.* AS SOON AS SCHOOL WAS OUT, I'D GET A SPOT WITH A GOOD VIEW AND EAGERLY WAIT FOR THE SHOW TO START. I USED TO THINK, "THIS OLD MAN DREW THE PICTURES HIMSELF." BUT ONE DAY, I COULDN'T WAIT TO SEE THE NEXT PART OF THE STORY SO I FOLLOWED THE OLD MAN WHEN HE WENT HOME ON HIS BICYCLE. BUT HE WAS SO FAST I COULDN'T CATCH UP WITH HIM. MAYBE THE REASON I BECAME A MANGA ARTIST WAS THE OLD MAN AND HIS KAMI-SHIBAI SHOW.

-KAZUKI TAKAHASHI, 2001

**KAMI-SHIBAI* IS AN OLD FORM OF JAPANESE STORYTELLING IN WHICH THE PERFORMER SLIPS DRAWINGS IN AND OUT OF A TV-SCREEN-LIKE BOX WHILE SPEAKING THE DIALOGUE AND SOUND EFFECTS.

Artist/author Kazuki Takahashi first tried to break into the manga business in 1982, but success eluded him until **Yu-Gi-Oh!** debuted in the Japanese **Weekly Shonen Jump** magazine in 1996. **Yu-Gi-Oh!**'s themes of friendship and fighting, together with Takahashi's weird and wonderful art, soon became enormously successful, spawning a real-world card game, video games, and two anime series. A lifelong gamer, Takahashi enjoys Shogi (Japanese chess), Mahjong, card games, and tabletop RPGs, among other games.

YU-GI-OH!: DUELIST VOL. 18
The SHONEN JUMP Manga Edition

STORY AND ART BY
KAZUKI TAKAHASHI

Translation & English Adaptation/Joe Yamazaki
Touch-up Art & Lettering/Eric Erbes
Design/Andrea Rice
Editor/Jason Thompson

Managing Editor/Frances E. Wall
Editorial Director/Elizabeth Kawasaki
Vice President & Editor in Chief/Yumi Hoashi
Sr. Director of Acquisitions/Rika Inouye
Sr. VP of Marketing/Liza Coppola
Exec. VP of Sales & Marketing/John Easum
Publisher/Hyoe Narita

In the original Japanese edition, YU-GI-OH!, YU-GI-OH!: DUELIST and YU-GI-OH!: MILLENNIUM WORLD are known collectively as YU-GI-OH!. The English YU-GI-OH!: DUELIST was originally volumes 8-31 of the Japanese YU-GI-OH!.

Printed in the U.S.A.

Published by VIZ Media, LLC
P.O. Box 77010
San Francisco, CA 94107

SHONEN JUMP Manga Edition
10 9 8 7 6 5 4 3 2 1
First printing, December 2006

www.viz.com

SHONEN JUMP MANGA

Vol. 18

THE POWER OF RA!

STORY AND ART BY

KAZUKI TAKAHASHI

THE STORY SO FAR...

YUGI MUTOU/
YU-GI-OH

When 10th grader Yugi solved the Millennium Puzzle, another spirit took up residence in his body...Yu-Gi-Oh, the King of Games, a dark avenger who challenges evildoers to "Shadow Games" of life and death!

YUGI FACES DEADLY ENEMIES!

Using his gaming skills, Yugi fights ruthless adversaries like Maximillion Pegasus, multimillionaire creator of the collectible card game "Duel Monsters," and Ryo Bakura, whose friendly personality turns evil when he is possessed by the spirit of the Millennium Ring. But Yugi's greatest rival is Seto Kaiba, the world's second-greatest gamer—and the ruthless teenage president of Kaiba Corporation. At first, Kaiba and Yugi are bitter enemies, but after fighting against a common adversary—Pegasus—they come to respect one another. But for all his powers, there is one thing Yu-Gi-Oh cannot do: remember who he is and where he came from.

HIROTO HONDA

ANZU MAZAKI

KATSUYA JONOUCHI

MARIK

ISHIZU ISHTAR

SETO KAIBA

THE TABLET OF THE PHARAOH'S MEMORIES

Then one day, when an Egyptian museum exhibit comes to Japan, Yugi sees an ancient carving of himself as an Egyptian pharaoh! The curator of the exhibit, Ishizu Ishtar, explains that there are seven Millennium Items, which were made to fit into a stone tablet in a hidden shrine in Egypt. According to the legend, when the seven Items are brought together, the pharaoh will regain his memories of his past life.

THE EGYPTIAN GOD CARDS

But Ishizu has a message for Kaiba as well. Ishizu needs Kaiba's help to win back two of three Egyptian God Cards—the rarest cards on Earth—from the clutches of the "Rare Hunters," a criminal syndicate led by the evil Marik, Ishizu's brother. In order to draw out the thieves, Kaiba announces "Battle City," an enormous "Duel Monsters" tournament. As the tournament rages, Yugi, Kaiba and Marik struggle for possession of the God Cards, ending up with one apiece. At last, eight finalists make it to the second stage of the tournament aboard Kaiba's blimp. To catch the heroes off-guard, Marik disguises himself as a duelist named "Namu," while his henchman Rishid pretends to be Marik himself. Now, the false Marik is locked in combat with Yugi's best friend Jonouchi. It'll take a miracle for Jonouchi to win...!

Vol. 18

CONTENTS

Duel 156 The Proof of the Clan!	7
Duel 157 God's Judgment!	27
Duel 158 Darkness Awakens!	47
Duel 159 One Duelist	67
Duel 160 The Dark Game!	87
Duel 161 The Unbreakable Duelist	107
Duel 162 Descent of the God!	127
Duel 163 The Rise of Ra!	147
Duel 164 The Depths of Darkness!	167
Master of the Cards	186
Previews	189

RISHID, MY SERVANT... MY SHADOW...

DESTROY ALL THE ENEMIES THAT STAND IN OUR WAY!!

HWOOOOOO

KILL JONOUCHI IN MY NAME!

DUEL 156: THE PROOF OF THE CLAN!

MARIK (RISHID)
Life Points 1600

JONOUCHI
Life Points 50

HWOOOO
DON'T GIVE UP, MAN...!
WHAT CAN HE DO...?
OKAY...
IT'S MY TURN...
MYSTICAL BEAST SELKET
Attack 4625
BABY DRAGON
Defense 700
JONO-UCHI...
GIVE UP YOUR HOPES OF DEFEATING ME...

HS
SS
THIS SCORPION THING, SELKET, KEEPS GROWING BY ABSORBING MY MONSTERS' ATTACK POINTS...
ITS ATTACK IS ALREADY OVER 4000...
SS
...
I DON'T HAVE ANY CARDS THAT CAN STOP IT...
RRG...
POLYMERIZATION
I'LL KEEP BABY DRAGON IN DEFENSE MODE...
AND END MY TURN...
FW
P
YOU INSIST ON DUELING, DESPITE THE FACT THAT YOU HAVE NO CHANCE...
I'LL FIGHT...
EVEN IF IT'S USELESS...
...UNTIL MY LIFE HITS ZERO!

I RESPECT YOUR SPIRIT...

...!

GWOOOO
KAT-SUYA...
YUGI...I'M SURE YOU KNOW...
NO MATTER HOW MUCH *FRIENDSHIP* AND *PERSEVERANCE* A DUELIST HAS IN HIS HEART...
THERE'S SOME TIMES WHEN YOU JUST CAN'T WIN...
AND THIS DUEL...
LOOKS LIKE ONE OF THEM...

MAI...
LOOK AT HIS *EYES!*
...!

BRING IT ON!!

...!!

WH- WHAT'S THAT LOOK...?

THERE'S NOTHING HE CAN DO...

BUT HIS EYES STILL HAVE FIGHTING SPIRIT...

SELKET, ATTACK!
KRUNCH
MUNCH
EAT THE BABY DRAGON!
AND GROW!
GULP
KRUNCH
BECOME EVEN STRONGER!
MYSTICAL BEAST SELKET
Attack
5225
NOW, JONOUCHI...
IT'S YOUR TURN...
YOUR LAST TURN...

THERE'S NOTHING I CAN DO....
TURN END...

JONO-UCHI...
...

IT'S ALL OVER...
WHEN SELKET ATTACKS ON THE NEXT TURN, JONOUCHI IS FINISHED...

AT THIS POINT, JONOUCHI'S CHANCES ARE ZERO PERCENT!
GOOD JOB...
YOU DID IT, RISHID! YOU WIN!

"WHAT CAN YOU SHOW..."
"BUT YOU CAN'T SEE...?"

WHAT ...?
...!?

I GOT A FUNNY FEELING...
I CAN'T EXPLAIN IT...
A LITTLE WHILE AGO, REACHED THE POINT WHERE I WAS RESIGNED TO LOSING...

AND JUST THEN...
WHEN WINNING OR LOSING DIDN'T MATTER...
IT'S LIKE...
I *SAW* SOMETHING I COULDN'T SEE BEFORE...

!

WHY DIDN'T I FIGURE IT OUT SOONER?
MUST HAVE BEEN THE HEAT OF BATTLE...
BUT THEN I REMEMBERED YUGI'S WORDS...
WHAT CAN YOU SHOW...
BUT YOU CAN'T SEE?

MARIK BRAIN-WASHED ME!
HE FORCED ME TO FIGHT A DUEL TO THE DEATH...
A POINTLESS BATTLE THAT ONLY HURT ME AND YUGI'S HEARTS!

I'LL NEVER FORGIVE HIM FOR THAT!

THEN GO AHEAD AND CURSE ME.
BUT...NO MATTER HOW GREAT YOUR ANGER...
YOU STILL CANNOT DEFEAT ME...

WHEN THIS DUEL STARTED...
I REALLY HATED YOU! I HATED YOUR GUTS!
BUT...
AS THE DUEL WENT ON...I LOST THAT HATRED...
AND I TRIED TO REMEMBER...
HOW BAD IT FELT WHEN MARIK TOOK OVER MY MIND...

YOU'RE A TRUE DUELIST WHO FOUGHT ME FAIR AND SQUARE!

FWP

SO FAIR THAT I FORGOT THOSE BAD MEMORIES!

BUT YOU...

BANG

'CAUSE YOU'RE NOT MARIK!

...!

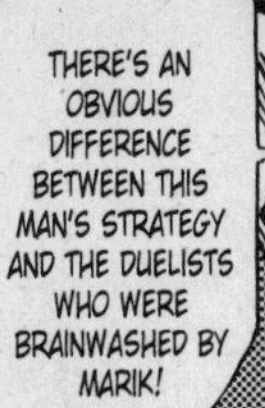
THERE'S AN OBVIOUS DIFFERENCE BETWEEN THIS MAN'S STRATEGY AND THE DUELISTS WHO WERE BRAINWASHED BY MARIK!

THEN WHERE'S THE REAL MARIK...?

HE'S NOT MARIK...!?
SO HE'S NOT THE WIELDER OF RA?!

AN ENEMY YOU CAN SHOW BUT YOU CAN'T SEE...
SO THE TRUE ENEMY IS ELSEWHERE...

OR...

IS THERE AN EIGHTH DUELIST...WE HAVEN'T SEEN YET...?

G' G'
IF THIS GOES ON, IT WILL BE... INCON-VENIENT...
G'

RRG...

IN A DUEL, NO ONE LISTENS TO THE LAST WORDS OF A LOSER!
EVERY-THING ENDS ON THIS TURN!!
SELKET THE SCORPION GOD! EAT HIM ALIVE!
D-D-D
!!
JONOUCHI
Life Points 50
SORRY YUGI...
THIS IS AS FAR AS I GO!!
WAIT!! RISHID!!
VOOM

DON'T KILL HIM YET!
MASTER MARIK...!
BA
BAM
WHY...?
STOP
...
HUH?
...!?
HE HAS TO DIE...
...BY THE HAND OF RA!!!

ZM
ZM
ZM
BUT... MY LORD...

TO MAINTAIN OUR DECEPTION... YOU MUST DEMONSTRATE THAT YOU POSSESS THE GOD CARD.
YOU ARE MARIK... DO YOU UNDER-STAND?!

SUMMON RA FROM WITHIN THE ARK IN THE TEMPLE!
THE COUNTERFEIT GOD CARD...

RISHID...IF YOU ARE A TRUE MEMBER OF THE CLAN OF THE TOMB GUARDIANS, YOUR HEART WILL ALLOW YOU TO CONTROL THE FAKE GOD CARD...
YOUR WILL IS STRONG! EVEN THOUGH MY VOICE REACHES YOU THROUGH THE POWER OF THE MILLENNIUM ROD, I CANNOT BRAINWASH YOU!
THAT IS PROOF THAT YOU ARE A TOMB GUARDIAN!

IF YOU CAN CONTROL THE COUNTERFEIT GOD CARD...
MY LATE FATHER WILL ACCEPT YOU AS HIS SON...
YOU WILL BE AS MUCH HIS HEIR AS I AM!
YOUR...
FATHER...
"BUT YOU'RE JUST A SERVANT!"
BUT... I...
I DO NOT BEAR THE BLOOD OF THE CLAN...
SUMMON RA...THAT WILL BE PROOF...
DO IT, RISHID...
!!

GYOOOOOO

!?

THE GOD CARD RA?!

THEN...HE IS MARIK...THE POSSESSOR OF RA...

WHAT...?!

RIGHT NOW, THE GOD CARD IS RESTING IN THE HOLY ARK...
THOUGH I MUST SACRIFICE ***MYSTICAL BEAST SELKET*** AND HALF MY LIFE POINTS TO OPEN THE LID...
G-G-G-
WHEN IT IS OPENED...THE ***SUN DRAGON RA*** WILL BE UNLEASHED!
G-G-G-
G-G-G-
!!
I GIVE UP HALF MY LIFE! AND SELKET AS WELL!
G-G-
G-
SOUL OF THE GOD WHICH SLEEPS IN THE ARK...
RISE AND SHOW YOURSELF!!
G-
G-

COME FORTH! SUN DRAGON RA!
G-G-
G-G-G
THE SUN DRAGON RA
???
ATK/??? DEF/???

THE SUN DRAGON RA...!
!!
I-IT'S REAL!

Duel 157: God's Judgment!

G-
G-
G-
G-
RA, COME FORTH!
G-G-G-

DUEL 157: GOD'S JUDGMENT!
D-D-D-D

ZAP
G-G-G-!!
G-G-G-
!
!
G-
G-
THE SUN DRAGON RA!
G-
THE THIRD GOD CARD! AT LAST!
G-

JONOUCHI
Life Points 50

RISHID, YOU'VE DONE WELL! YOU CONTROLLED THE COUNTERFEIT GOD!
THIS PROVES THAT YOU HAVE THE SAME BLOOD AS A TRUE ISHTAR!

NO ONE WILL DOUBT THAT YOU ARE A GOD CARD WIELDER WHEN THEY SEE RA IN FRONT OF THEM!
NOW I CAN CARRY OUT MY PLAN...

MY PLAN TO FIND SETO KAIBA'S SECRET...

WHY IS THERE A FIGURE WHO LOOKS LIKE KAIBA ON THE ANCIENT MURAL FROM THE KING'S MORTUARY TEMPLE...?

AND WHY...
IS AN ITEM SIMILAR TO THE MILLENNIUM ROD IN HIS HAND...?

IF I CAN READ HIS MEMORY, I MAY BE ABLE TO SOLVE BOTH MYSTERIES...

THIS IS THE END!
!
FAREWELL, JONOUCHI!

G-
WHAT?!
G-
G-
G-

THROB
THROB

THROB
WHAT...?!

THE REAL GOD...

INSIDE MY DECK...IS EMITTING AN AURA OF ANGER...!

G-
G-
G-
G-
G-

G
G
G
G
G
...!?
SHOOM
WHY?
WHY ISN'T GOD ATTACKING...?
SHOOM
...!?
G
G
G
RA IS TURNING INTO A BLACK MIST...
G
G
G
G
G
G
G

GWOOOOOOOO
MMMMW
WHAT IS THIS...?!
...
...NO...
THIS ISN'T RA...!
G- GG G-

G" G" G" G"

FLASH

THIS IS GOD'S WRATH FOR USING A COPY...!!

GW ODDDDD !!

WH- WHAT THE...!!

HEY! TELL ME! WHAT'S GOING ON?!

KAKOOM
WHOA!
BLAM
BLAM
BLAM
!!
ERG...
BLAM
RA IS STRIKING DOWN THE PLAYERS OF THE GAME...!
JONO-UCHI! LOOK OUT!
KATS-UYA!!

GOD...DO YOU NOT ACCEPT ME AS A SUCCESSOR OF THE CLAN...?
ARE YOU SAYING I DO NOT HAVE THE RIGHT TO COMMAND YOU...?
GOD...IS THIS YOUR JUDGMENT ON ME?!
KA
B
GAM

B-BMP
RISHID...
WHAM
BMP
RISHID!!
BLAM
BLAM
RRG...
JONO...

KA-BLAM
...!
JONO-UCHI!

THEY BOTH HAVE LIFE POINTS LEFT.
EVEN IF THAT LAST ATTACK HURT THEM PERSONALLY, THEIR POINTS IN THE GAME WERE UNTOUCHED!

STEP BACK! THE DUEL ISN'T OVER YET!
ARE YOU CRAZY?! THEY'RE BOTH DOWN!!

KATS-UYA!
DASH
JONO-UCHI!

JONOUCHI
Life Points 50
MARIK (RISHID)
Life Points 800

PLEASE GET UP!
WHAT ...?!
JONO-UCHI!

WHO WINS THE DUEL THEN?!
WHO-EVER STANDS UP FIRST ON THIS TURN...
WHOEVER DISPLAYS THE GREATER WILLINGNESS TO CONTINUE...THEY WILL BE DEEMED THE WINNER...

...
JONO-UCHI!
GRAA...

RRG...
NGH...

...
...!
M-MASTER MARIK...

NO... DON'T DO IT...
DO NOT AWAKEN... HIM...

GGH...
GRR...

AS LONG AS I'M HERE...I CAN RESTRAIN THE MASTER'S TRUE HATRED...

NGH...

IF I FALL...HIS DARK SIDE...WILL ONCE AGAIN BE AWAKENED...

WAKE UP! WAKE UP!

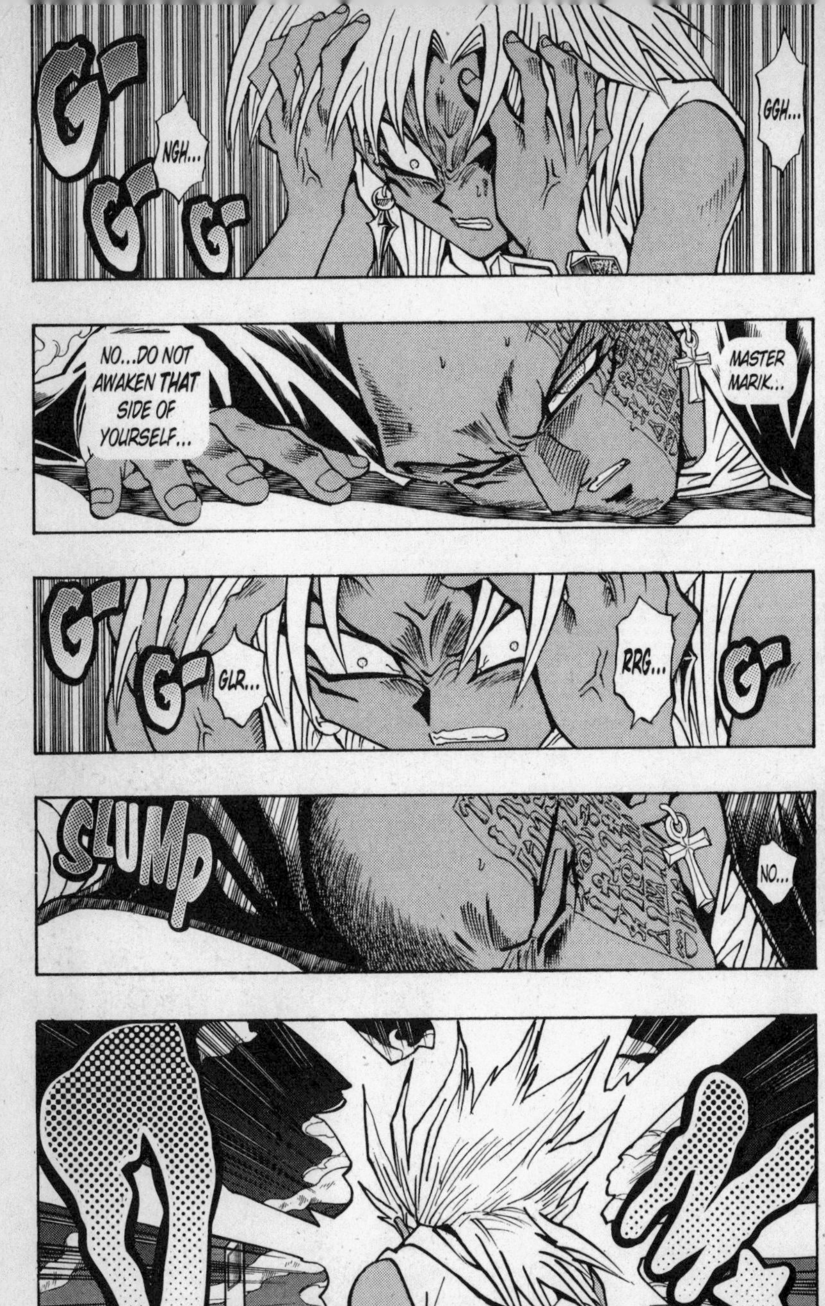

Duel 158: Darkness Awakens!

G-G-G-G-G
DUEL 158: DARKNESS AWAKENS!

HYOOOO
OOOO

SO YOU FAILED TO COMMAND GOD... YOU NEVER HAD THE BLOOD OF OUR CLAN...

SHH--

JONO-UCHI...

SHH--

...

JONO-UCHI! WAKE UP!
C'MON MAN! GET UP!
SNR--RK
NN
GET YOUR BUTT UP!
...
...NNH...
YOU'VE BEEN SLEEPING SINCE FIFTH PERIOD!
HUH...?
IS IT ALREADY TIME FOR MY PAPER ROUTE...?
STOP SLEEP TALKING! SCHOOL'S ALREADY OVER!
YAWN...
...I'M SLEEPY...

JONOUCHI! DID YOU FORGET WHAT DAY IT IS?
TODAY'S THE DAY OF THE DUEL MONSTERS TOURNAMENT AT DOMINO TOYSAURUS!
WH
AM!
!!
YIKES
TH-THAT'S RIGHT--!!
GRAB
...!
YOU'VE BEEN TALKING ABOUT BEING THE BEST IN TOWN!
I DIDN'T FORGET! HERE'S MY DECK!!
AND THE DUEL DISK'S IN HERE TOO!
DUDE... DON'T YOU HAVE ANYTHING IN YOUR SCHOOLBAG BESIDES YOUR LUNCH AND COLLECTIBLE CARD GAME GEAR?
SHUT UP!
A REAL DUELIST TRAVELS LIGHT!
HMPH.
!!
YOU SCRUB DUELIST...

WHAT'D YOU CALL ME?!
JONOUCHI! SAVE IT FOR THE DUEL!
GRR...
FUME
@#$% KAIBA! I'LL BEAT HIM ONE OF THESE DAYS!
C'MON!
WE DON'T HAVE MUCH TIME!
Y-YEAH!
EEP...
SCATTER
SORRY... GIMME A MINUTE...!
I DROPPED MY CARDS...!
...
YOU'RE SUCH A KLUTZ! THIS ISN'T 52 PICK-UP!
YEAH, YEAH, SORRY...!
LET'S PICK 'EM UP AND GO TO THE TOURNAMENT!

THERE! IS THAT ALL OF THEM?
LOOKS LIKE IT...
WAIT... LEMME CHECK MY DECK...
HMM... MM...
HEY, HURRY UP JONOUCHI!
THE TOURNAMENT'S GONNA START!
YEAH!
I'LL BE RIGHT THERE!

GWOOOOO

JONO-UCHI! YOU DID IT!
YUGI...
HONDA... EVERYBODY...
WHY AREN'T YOU AT DOMINO TOYSAURUS...?
YOU MORON! YOU WERE TALKING IN YOUR SLEEP!

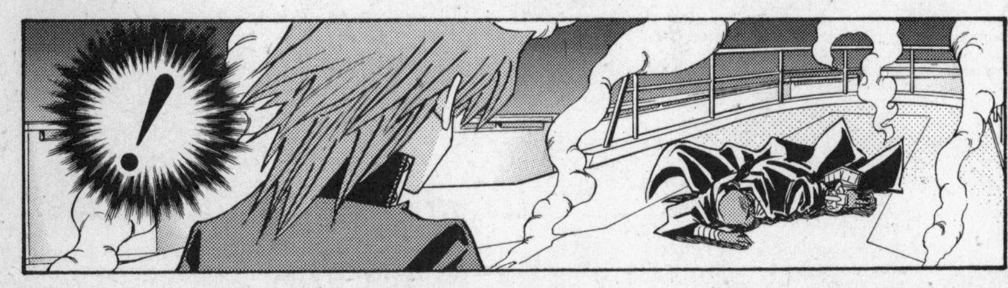

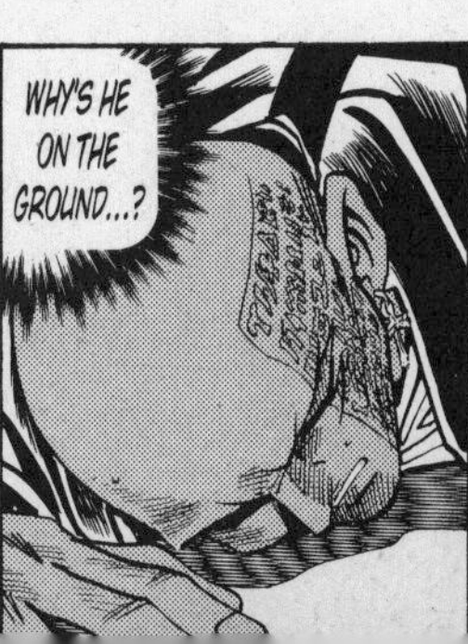

THE WINNER IS... KATSUYA JONO-UCHI!!

ME...?
I WON?!
WHOO HOO! YOU DID IT!
GOOD JOB, KATS-UYA!!

HMPH!
I CAN'T BELIEVE JONOUCHI WON...WHAT A DISGRACE...

BUT...WHY DIDN'T RA MATERIALIZE? INSTEAD BOTH PLAYERS WERE STRUCK DOWN...
AS IF A RAGING STORM STIRRED THE HEAVENS...

COULD THAT GOD CARD BE...
...A FAKE?
DASH

HEY!
HEY, WAKE UP!!
OOOO

...
UGH...

J-JONO-UCHI...
...I...AM PROUD TO HAVE... FOUGHT AGAINST...
YOU...

YEAH! ME TOO! YOU WERE A REAL DUELIST!!
DASH

HANG IN THERE!
YOU'RE NOT MARIK, ARE YOU?
WHO ARE YOU?! TELL ME!!

I AM...
...A SHADOW...

YUGI...
...PLEASE...
STOP... IT...
THAT MAN'S... OTHER...

!!
HANG IN THERE!!
...
THIS GUY WOULDN'T BRAINWASH ANYBODY...
GRR...
WHERE ARE YOU!? WHERE'S THE REAL MARIK WHO MADE THIS GUY FIGHT IN YOUR PLACE?!
HE IS MARIK!
OR AT LEAST... MARIK'S SHADOW...

BUT THE ONE WHO CASTS THAT SHADOW...
G
G
G
B'BMP
...IS ME!

HE'S MARIK!!
IT'S YOU! YOU BRAIN-WASHING CREEP!
YOU'RE DEAD MEAT!
MARIK...
THE POSSESSOR OF RA...
B-BMP
I NO LONGER...
NEED A SHADOW...
WHEN HE IS AROUND... I AM HIDDEN...
COMPARED TO ME, THE OTHER MARIK IS A CHILD...
THAT'S WHY HE CAN NEVER... FINISH A DUEL... PROPERLY...
B-BMP
ANOTHER MARIK...?!
HE HAS ANOTHER PERSONALITY!!
IF I HAD TO MENTION ONE OBVIOUS DIFFERENCE...
HE'S AFRAID OF THE DARK...

BUT I LOVE IT...
KEH KEH...

KAIBA'S MEMO-RIES...?!
COULD THAT FIGURE ON THE MURAL BE...
I'M SURE WE'LL FIND OUT SOON ENOUGH...
SHF
KEH KEH KEH...
SHF

DUEL DI
GWOOOOOOOOO

FINALLY...

MARIK'S DARK SIDE HAS AWAKENED...

NO ONE CAN CHANGE THE COURSE OF THEIR DESTINY...

WE ARE HEADED TO A FUTURE OF DESPAIR...THE LAST FLICKERING LIGHT HAS BEEN LOST...

KEEEEEEN
BMP
BMP
YUGI...THE MILLENNIUM BATTLE HAS FINALLY BEGUN...

WE ARE HEADED FOR THE TRUE DARKNESS...
SHOOOOO
AND NONE OF US CAN TURN BACK...

THE BATTLE CITY TOURNAMENT!

YUGI MUTOU!

KATSUYA JONOUCHI!

SO FAR, TWO DUELISTS HAVE ADVANCED TO THE SEMI-FINALS...

OUT OF THE FOUR REMAINING DUELISTS, TWO WILL MAKE IT TO THE SEMI-FINALS...

WHO WILL DUEL NEXT...?

DUEL 159: ONE DUELIST

Duel 159: One Duelist

MEDICAL ROOM

MARIK'S THE ONE I'M REALLY MAD AT!
THAT #$%@&#%!
MAKING THIS GUY ACT LIKE HIS "SHADOW," AND THEN JUST ABANDONING HIM...

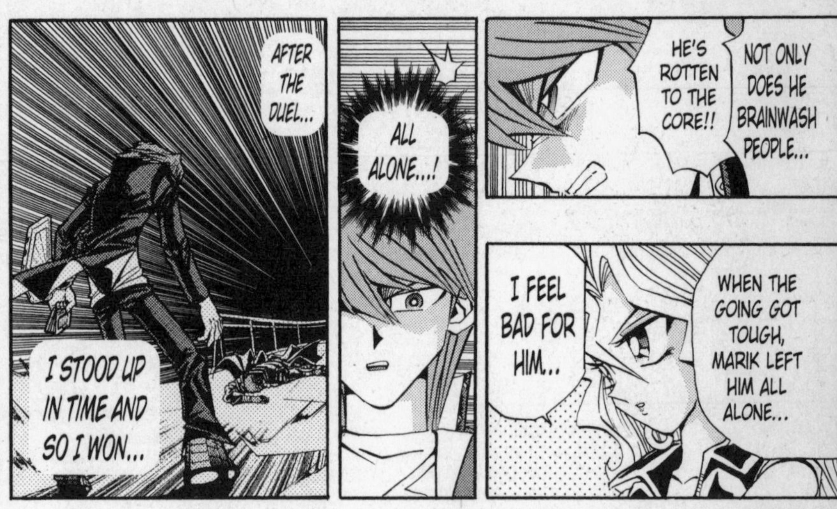

NOT ONLY DOES HE BRAINWASH PEOPLE...
HE'S ROTTEN TO THE CORE!!
WHEN THE GOING GOT TOUGH, MARIK LEFT HIM ALL ALONE...
I FEEL BAD FOR HIM...
ALL ALONE...!
AFTER THE DUEL...
I STOOD UP IN TIME AND SO I WON...

THIS GUY... AND ME...
I THINK I KNOW WHAT DECIDED OUR DUEL...

...?
I HAD A DREAM...
OF YOU GUYS...
SPIR

I HAD FRIENDS WAITING FOR ME...
BUT HE...
MUST HAVE BEEN ALL ALONE...
SPIRIT
THANKS, YOU GUYS...
YOU GAVE ME STRENGTH...
...
WELL...
YOU DON'T HAVE TO THANK US, JUST PAY ME BACK FOR THE BEEF BOWL I BOUGHT YOU!
WHY BRING THAT UP *NOW?!*
FRIENDS, HUH...?
LET'S GO, HE'S IN GOOD HANDS NOW!
MEDICAL ROOM
THE LOTTERY FOR THE NEXT DUEL'S ABOUT TO START!

HEY! HEY JONOUCHI!
CAN I ASK YOU SOME-THING?
HUH...?
WHAT IS IT, MAI?

THE DREAM YOU SAW...
EH?
I WAS IN IT TOO, RIGHT?
YOU KNOW... WAS I IN IT?

MM...
OH CRAP...

W-WELL... YOU KNOW...
MY DREAM TOOK PLACE IN OUR CLASSROOM...
SO OF COURSE YOU WEREN'T IN IT!
YOU'RE TOO OLD TO BE IN HIGH SCHOOL!

WHAT DID YOU SAY?!
MAYBE NEXT TIME...
YEAH! YOU CAN PLAY THE TEACHER!!
...!
THAT IDIOT...

MAI!
THE NEXT DUEL MIGHT BE YOURS!
WIN IT!

...
SURE...

....

OW! LET GO!
GRR...! YOU IDIOT!
SPIRIT

WHAT WAS THAT FOR, ANZU?
YOU'RE THE WORST!!

HUH?

HEH...

WHAT'S WRONG WITH ME...?

UNTIL I MET THESE GUYS....I ALWAYS FOUGHT BY MYSELF...
WITHOUT ANYBODY'S HELP...I STOOD ALONE!
THAT WAS MY PRIDE AND MY BELIEF...!!
KLANG
THERE CAN BE ONLY ONE WINNER...
THE WORLD'S A HARSH PLACE. I DON'T HAVE TIME TO LICK OTHER PEOPLE'S WOUNDS...!
AFTER ALL...
I'M A DUELIST!!

AND NOW...WE WILL DECIDE THE MATCH-UP FOR THE THIRD ROUND OF THE TOURNAMENT!

BAM

D-D-D-
ULTIMATE BINGO MACHINE, GO!!!
TONK
BONK
BONK
1
3
6
8

KLATTA★

THIRD DUEL! THE FIRST DUELIST IS...

NO. 6! MAI KUJAKU!

BA

NG★

STEP
...!
WAIT, MAI! YOUR OPPONENT'S NOT DECIDED YET!
NO MATTER WHO THEY ARE, I'LL WIN!
YUGI!
JONO-UCHI!
I'LL SEE YOU IN THE SEMI-FINALS!

I'M NOT A SOFT DUELIST LIKE YOU!!
WHAT?!
GRRR
WHAT'D YOU SAY?!
I DARE YOU TO SAY THAT AGAIN!
JONO-UCHI...
SEE YA!
GRR...
FINE THEN...!
BONK
BONK
BA
THE NEXT DUELIST IS--...

KLIK
ONE BY ONE...
I'LL SACRIFICE THEM TO THE DARKNESS...
RISHID...
THE SEAL YOU CARVED IN YOUR FACE KEPT MY *HATRED* IN CHECK...
AS LONG AS YOU'RE ALIVE...
THERE'S ALWAYS THE RISK THAT YOU'LL WAKE UP...AND *RETURN* ME TO THE DARKNESS...

G-
G-
G-
NOW IT'S YOUR TURN TO BE IN THE DARK... FOREVER...
READ THIS WAY
THE SECOND DUELIST OF THE THIRD ROUND IS...
...MARIK ISHTAR!
WSH
KEH KEH...I'LL KEEP YOU ALIVE FOR A WHILE LONGER...

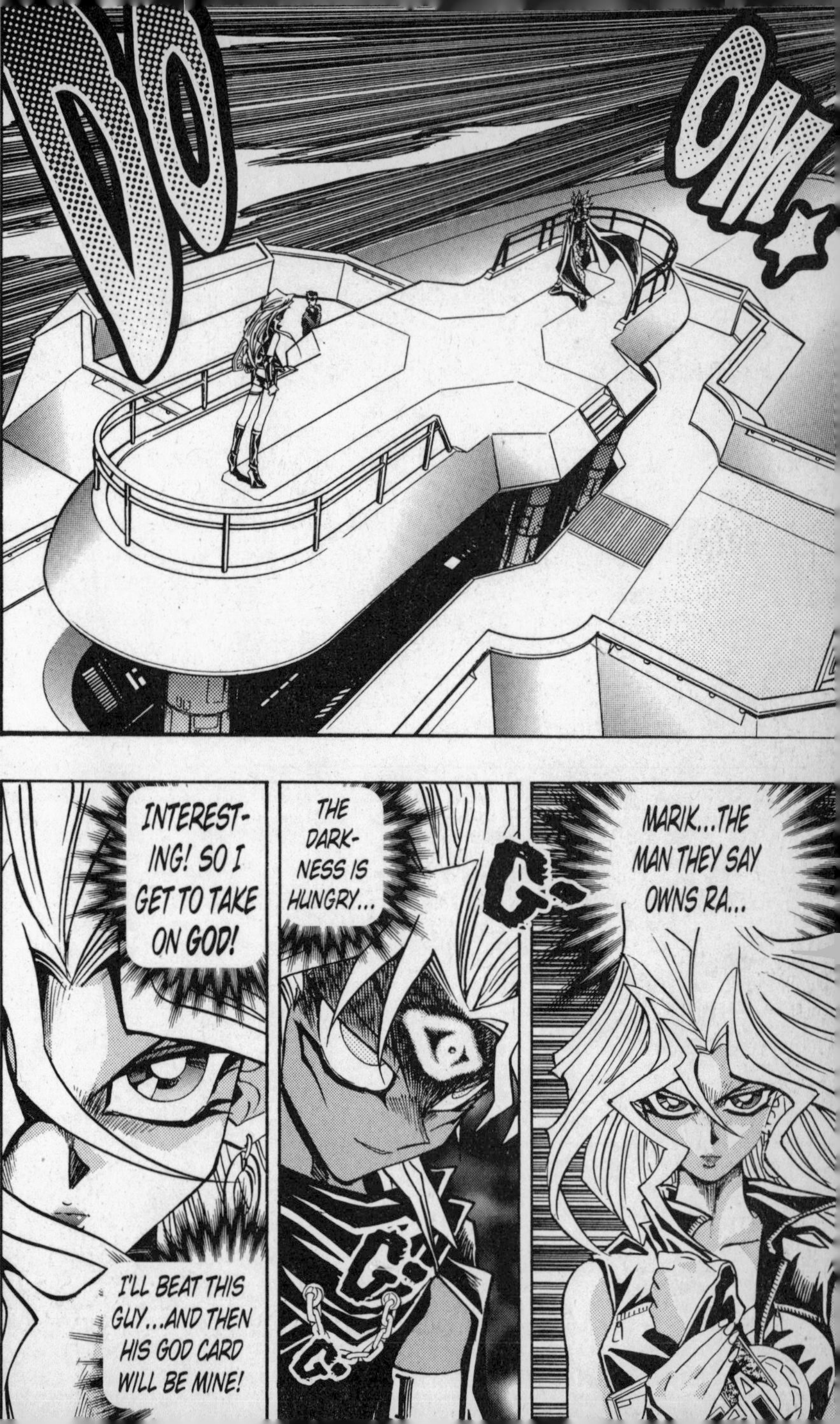

DO
OM

MARIK...THE MAN THEY SAY OWNS RA...

G

THE DARKNESS IS HUNGRY...

G

G

INTERESTING! SO I GET TO TAKE ON GOD!

I'LL BEAT THIS GUY...AND THEN HIS GOD CARD WILL BE MINE!

MAI KUJAKU VS. MARIK ISHTAR!

GWOOOOOO

DUEL!!!

FWAP

G- G- G-

GWMM
GWMM
...!

WHAT'S GOING ON?!

FEELS LIKE I CAN'T BREATHE...
IS THIS... FEAR?
AM I AFRAID OF HIM ALREADY...?
C'MON, MAI! WIN IT!
BEAT MARIK!!
!!
YOU GUYS...

Duel 160: The Dark Game!!

GWM
GWMMM
MAI KUJAKU VS. MARIK ISHTAR!
...!

HWOO
OO
...
I THOUGHT I TOLD YOU NOT TO INTERFERE, YUGI!!
I FIGHT ALONE!!
SHEESH! STOP ACTING TOUGH FOR ONCE!
WE KNOW YOU'RE A REAL DUELIST...
BUT MORE THAN THAT...
...YOU'RE OUR FRIEND!
...
HMPH...
DO WHAT YOU WANT!

YOUR FRIEND, EH...?
WELL THEN...YOU CAN WATCH AS I DESTROY HER IN FRONT OF YOUR EYES...!
GWM
WHAT THE...?
THIS BLACK FOG IS GATHERING AROUND THE DUELING PLATFORM!
IT'S GETTING HARD TO BREATHE, TOO! AT FIRST I THOUGHT THE AIR WAS THIN BECAUSE WE'RE SO HIGH UP...
IT'S LIKE THERE'S A FOG **CORK** DOWN OUR THROATS...
IF IT GETS ANY THICKER, WE WON'T EVEN BE ABLE TO **SEE** THEM!
...!
THIS IS...
...A SHADOW GAME!
THAT'S RIGHT, YUGI...SO YOU FIGURED IT OUT...
WHAT'S GATHERING AROUND US IS **HATRED**...A HATRED DARKER THAN THE DARKEST NIGHT...

THIS IS THE SIGN THAT THE **SHADOW GAMES** ARE ABOUT TO BEGIN...

THAT'S A MILLEN-NIUM ITEM IN MARIK'S HAND...!

WHAT'S HE GOING TO DO WITH IT?!

MARIK!

DON'T DO THIS!

THIS DARK CLOUD IS NOTHING LESS THAN MY OWN **HATE**...MY DESIRE FOR **REVENGE**...

GWM

GWM

GWM

IT WILL NEVER LIFT UNTIL I KILL YUGI AND DRAG HIM DOWN INTO IT...INTO THE DARK...

THE DARKNESS IS HUNGRY, YUGI...

AS A **SACRIFICE**, I'LL GIVE IT **THIS GIRL!**

DO YOU THINK I'M AN AMATEUR, YUGI!?
ONCE A DUELIST ACCEPTS A DUEL...
...IF THEY GIVE UP AND TURN THEIR BACK TO THE ENEMY...A PART OF THEIR HEART WILL DIE FOREVER!
...!
MAI...
YOU SHOULD KNOW THAT BETTER THAN ANYBODY ELSE!
LISTEN, YUGI!
YOU TOO, JONOUCHI!
I'LL WIN THIS DUEL NO MATTER WHAT HAPPENS!
SO THAT I CAN FIGHT YOU GUYS NEXT!
TCH...
THEN DO IT!
BEAT HIM, MAI! THAT'S THE MAI KUJAKU I KNOW!
YES... THAT'S RIGHT, WOMAN...
GRAB LIFE BY THE THROAT! SCREAM YOUR BATTLE CRY! AND I'LL MAKE YOU SCREAM FOR REAL...
I'M GOING TO DEVOUR YOU...SPICE IT WITH YOUR PRIDE!
BA-BUMP

YUGI...
...
WE CAN'T STOP HER FROM DOING THIS...CAN WE?
MAI! YOU HAVE TO WIN!

HERE I COME, MARIK!
GWM
GWM
GWM
MAI KUJAKU
Life Points 4000
MARIK ISHTAR
Life Points 4000

THE SHADOW GAME BEGINS!
GWM
GWM

C'MON, MAI! TAKE HIM DOWN!
GWM
GWM
YOU CAN DO IT, MAI!
WHAT IS THIS SHADOW GAME HE'S CASTING...?
MAI...BE CAREFUL!
FWP
I GO FIRST!

D-D-D
I PLAY... AMAZONESS SWORDS WOMAN!!
IN ATTACK MODE!
D
AMAZONESS SWORDS WOMAN ★★★★
ATK/1500 DEF/1600
AND I ALSO PLAY...
...A FACE-DOWN CARD ON THE BOARD!
TURN END!
WHAM
GWM GWMM
KEH KEH...MAI KUJAKU...
GWMM
YOU DIDN'T KNOW IT BEFORE NOW...BUT YOU ARE PLAYING A SHADOW GAME.
DO YOU SEE THE LINE STRETCHING FROM YOUR BODY...?

WHAT IS THIS...!?
NO! IT'S...
...!!
IT'S CONNECTED TO MY MONSTER... WHAT IS THIS STRING...!?
BAM
BA- BA-

AND MORE THAN THAT...YOU'LL FEEL *PLEASURE* UNLIKE ANYTHING YOU HAVE EVER EXPERIENCED...

KEH KEH KEH...

IT'S MY TURN...

THIS MAN MARIK...HE HAS THE EYES OF A MADMAN!

MAKYURA THE DESTRUCTOR!
MAKYURA THE DESTRUCTOR ★★★★
During the turn this card is sent to the Graveyard, the owner of this card can activate Trap Card(s) from his/her hand.
ATK/1600 DEF/1200
YOU SEE THAT I, TOO...
...HAVE A LIFE LINE BETWEEN MY MONSTER AND MYSELF...

MAI KUJAKU...I'LL LET YOU ENJOY THE WORLD OF SHADOWS WHICH ONLY WE DUELISTS CAN SEE...

MAKYURA ATTACKS!

HERE HE COMES!!

DIE!!
AMAZONESS SWORDS WOMAN Attack 1500
MAKYURA THE DESTRUCTOR Attack 1600
HEH...
HE FELL FOR IT!!
FLIP
TRAP CARD, ACTIVATE!
AMAZONESS ARCHERS!!
AMAZONESS ARCHERS
All monsters on your opponent's side of the field become face-up Attack Position and as long as they remain face-up on the field decrease their ATK by 500 points.
KEH KEH...

SHOOM
SHOOM
GWAA...
THOK
TH-THOK
THIS TRAP CARD KEEPS YOUR MONSTER FROM MOVING...
...AND LOWERS ITS ATTACK VALUE BY 500 POINTS!
NOW, MY AMAZON-ESS! FIGHT BACK!

SLASH
AMAZON DECAPITATION STRIKE!
GYO-OO...
I GOT HIM...
FSSHHH
UNGH...
...
WHAT?!

KEH KEH...
BAM
NICE HIT...
NICE FOR ME, THAT IS...
YEE...
MARIK'S HEAD IS...!!
GRAB
EEYA-AA!!!
I'M AFRAID MAKYURA THE DESTRUCTOR HAS A SPECIAL ABILITY...
WHEN IT'S DEFEATED, I CAN INSTANTLY PLAY A TRAP CARD FROM MY HAND...
LET'S SEE... WHICH CARD SHALL I CHOOSE...
GYAA!!! HIS HEAD!!!
WHAT'S GOING ON?! MAI!
THAT SCREAM WASN'T NORMAL...

WHY'S SHE SCREAMING? LOOKS LIKE A NORMAL DUEL TO ME!

KYAAAA!

MISS MAI!

MAI! PULL YOURSELF TOGETHER!!

I'LL ACTIVATE THIS TRAP CARD, **ROPE OF LIFE.**

THIS CARD TAKES EFFECT ON A MONSTER WHO JUST DIED...

IT REVIVES IT WITH 800 EXTRA ATTACK POINTS AND ALLOWS IT TO ATTACK AGAIN...

G G G

THOUGH I HAVE TO LOSE ALL THE CARDS IN MY HAND...

BRR BRR

AAAH...

ROPE OF LIFE
[TRAP CARD]
When 1 of your monsters is sent to the Graveyard as a result of battle, discard your entire hand to activate this card. Special Summon the monster to the field, increasing the ATK of the monster by 800 points.

BRR BRR BRR

HEY... WHAT'RE YOU SO AFRAID OF?

IT WAS *YOU* WHO CUT OFF MY SLAVE'S HEAD...

AND YES, IT HURTS...

I'LL DOUBLE THE PAIN YOU GAVE ME...
GO... MAKYURA...
GWHH
CHOP
MAKYURA! EXECUTE HER!
MAKYURA THE DESTRUCTOR Attack 1500
AMAZONESS SWORDS WOMAN Attack 1900
BUTCHER THE SWORDS-WOMAN!
...!!

SPLR
...
RSSSH
MAI KUJAKU
Life Points 3600
...BLOOD...!?
HEY MAI! WHAT'S WRONG!?
MAI!
WHEN YOUR MONSTER IS DAMAGED, YOU ARE DAMAGED...
AND WHEN YOU LOSE 4,000 LIFE POINTS, YOU REALLY DIE...
IT IS AN ILLUSION...
BUT THE PAIN IS NOT...
THIS IS MY SHADOW GAME...
MARIK
Life Points 4000

!!
ZIOK
MAKYURA STRIKES, KILLING THE AMAZONESS SWORDS-WOMAN!
DUEL 161:
THE UNBREAKABLE DUELIST
BLOOD ...!!
...
STABB
UNGH...
WHAT...!? IT FEELS LIKE I WAS SLASHED IN THE CHEST...
THE MONSTER AND PLAYER ARE CONNECTED BY A LIFE LINE...
IF ONE IS HURT, SO IS THE OTHER...

Duel 161: The Unbreakable Duelist

READ THIS WAY

AGH...

MAI KUJAKU
Life Points 3600

...!!

HEY... SOMETHING'S WRONG WITH MAI...!

THE MOMENT HER MONSTER WAS DESTROYED...SHE FELL TO HER KNEES!

MAI! PULL YOURSELF TOGETHER!

YOU DIDN'T LOSE MUCH LIFE!

NNH...

...!

...

THIS IS NOTHING...
BY THE TIME THIS GAME IS OVER, I'LL TEAR HER APART...

MAI!
DON'T BE CONFUSED! IT'S JUST AN ILLUSION!

A WHAT?!
THIS PAIN...
THIS BLOOD...
IS AN ILLUSION...?

IN A SHADOW GAME, **WILLPOWER** IS THE KEY TO SUCCESS! DON'T LET HIM BREAK YOU!
THOSE ILLUSIONS ARE CREATED BY THE FEAR AND TERROR IN YOUR HEART!

FEAR...
TERROR...
STAND UP, MAI!
YOU CAN DO IT, MISS KUJAKU!

YOUR FRIENDSHIP SHINES IN MY HEART LIKE A RAY OF LIGHT!

NOW IT'S MY TURN!
GO! MAI!!
FWP
I PLAY AMAZONESS CHAIN MASTER IN ATTACK MODE!
DOOM
THEN I PLAY A FACE-DOWN CARD AND END MY TURN!

D D D D
MAKYURA THE DESTRUCTOR Attack 1900
AMAZONESS CHAIN MASTER Attack 1500
IT'S MY TURN...
HIS MAKYURA THE DESTRUCTOR IS STRONG ENOUGH TO DEFEAT MY AMAZONESS CHAIN MASTER...
HE SHOULD ATTACK RIGHT AWAY...
UNLESS HE'S AFRAID OF MY FACE-DOWN CARD...
...
BUT... MY TRAP ISN'T MY FACE-DOWN CARD...
IT'S THE CHAIN MASTER'S SPECIAL ABILITY!

WHEN AMAZON-ESS CHAIN MASTER GOES TO THE GRAVEYARD WHILE IN ATTACK MODE...HER "BRINK OF DEATH CHAIN DANCE" IS ACTIVATED...

BY PAYING 1000 OF MY LIFE POINTS, I CAN STEAL ONE CARD FROM MY OPPONENT'S DECK!

G

G

G

M

BA

THAT'S RIGHT...

THE SUN DRAGON RA

★★★★★★★★★★

???

ATK/??? DEF/???

BA

I'LL STEAL MARIK'S GOD CARD...!

I'LL TEACH YOU... OVER AND OVER...

THAT THE PAIN IS NOT AN ILLUSION...

GWOOO

OOO

MY CARD IS...

THIS WILL SUIT YOUR AMAZONESS CHAIN MASTER!
THE VISE DEMON... VISER DES!
D.D.D.D
VISER DES ★★★★
This monster is invincible for three turns after it is summoned.
ATK/500 DEF/?
D.D.D.D.
HE'S ATTACKING ME?! BUT HE ONLY HAS 500 ATTACK POINTS...!
!!

KLANG

!!

BUT...BUT IT HAD LESS ATTACK POINTS! WHY DIDN'T IT LOSE?

VISER DES CAPTURED THE CHAIN MASTER?!

BECAUSE OF ITS SPECIAL ABILITY...!

SKWEEK
SKWEEK
SKWEEK
SKWEEK
SKWEEK
AGH...
NGH...
SKWEEK
THE VISE SLOWLY CRUSHES YOUR HEAD...
"SKWEEK SKWEEK SKWEEK"... I'LL TAKE THREE TURNS BEFORE YOUR *BRAINS* RUN OUT OF YOUR *EARS*...
MAI KUJAKU... YOU'LL TASTE THE SAME PAIN AS YOUR MONSTER...
KHA HA HA HA!
AGGHH!
SKWEEK
SKWEEK
SKWEEK
SKWEEK
SKWEEK

READ THIS WAY
MAI!
WHAT'S GOING ON?! IS SHE EXPERIENCING THE SAME PAIN AS HER MONSTER?
MAI! GET A HOLD OF YOURSELF!!
GWMMM
GWMMM
KHA HA HA HA!
CURSES! MAI'S MIND IS COMPLETELY OVERWHELMED BY MARIK'S DARKNESS!
GG... GGHH...
SKWEEK
SKWEEK
SKWEEK
SKWEEK
G G
IF THIS DUEL GOES ON, MAI'S LIFE WILL...!
G
G

STOP HURTING HER!
MARIK!!
RMMM
NOW, NOW...
NO ONE CAN STOP A SHADOW GAME...
YUGI...
THIS WOMAN WILL DIE THE MOMENT I WIN...
YOU FILTHY...
RMMM
THAT'S RIGHT, YUGI!
YES!
HATE ME!
SAY MORE!
I'VE BEEN WAITING TO FIGHT YOU FOR 1,000 YEARS...
LET YOUR ANGER REACH OUT AND TOUCH MY OWN!

GRR...

YOU WON'T GET AWAY WITH THIS, MARIK...

KRIK

KRIK

GH...

KRIK

NH...

GG...

MAI!

YUGI...

THIS IS...

MY FIGHT...

STAY OUT OF IT...

MAI!

I'M A DUELIST...

I'LL FIGHT HIM TILL THE END!

I FLIP MY FACE-DOWN CARD!
SPELL CARD... GRAVE ARM!
...!
GRAVE ARM
[SPELL CARD]
Place any 1 monster in the Graveyard.
I'LL BURY ONE MONSTER WITH THIS SPELL CARD!
I'M SORRY...
THAT WON'T EFFECT VISER DES...
HEH...
WHO SAID ANYTHING ABOUT YOUR MONSTER?
...
I'M GOING TO BURY...

AMAZONESS CHAIN MASTER!!

D.D.D.

HMM...

SENDING YOUR OWN MONSTER TO THE GRAVE...

THAT'S RIGHT...

BUT!

THE CHAIN MASTER HAS A SPECIAL ABILITY!

SHWAAA
WSSHHH
HH
...
I GIVE UP 1000 LIFE POINTS...
TO TAKE ONE MONSTER FROM YOUR DECK!

YOUR GOD CARD!
THE SUN DRAGON RA
???
ATK/??? DEF/???
SHAA
AAAAA
BAM
HEH...
MAI KUJAKU
Life Points 2600
TORTURING YOU TO DEATH WON'T BE ENOUGH NOW...
WOMAN!
KEH...
YES!
WOW, MAI! YOU RULE!

THE SUN DRAGON RA
???
ATK/??? DEF/???

AMAZONESS CHAIN MASTER ACTIVATES HER LAST-DITCH POWER!
BRINK OF DEATH CHAIN DANCE!
Duel 162: Descent of the God!
YOUR GOD CARD... THE SUN DRAGON RA!
IT'S MINE NOW!!
THE SUN DRAGON RA
???
WOMAN...
YOUR SUFFERING WILL BE LEGENDARY... EVEN IN SHADOW GAMES!

SOUNDS LIKE FUN...
BUT BEFORE THAT...
YOU'LL BE DANCING IN HELL!

YEAH, WAY TO GO MAI!!
SHE MUST HAVE BEEN PLANNING TO STEAL HIS GOD CARD ALL ALONG!
GOOD JOB, MAI!!
NOW THAT YOU HAVE HIS GOD CARD, MARIK SHOULD BE CONSIDERABLY WEAKER!
KEH...

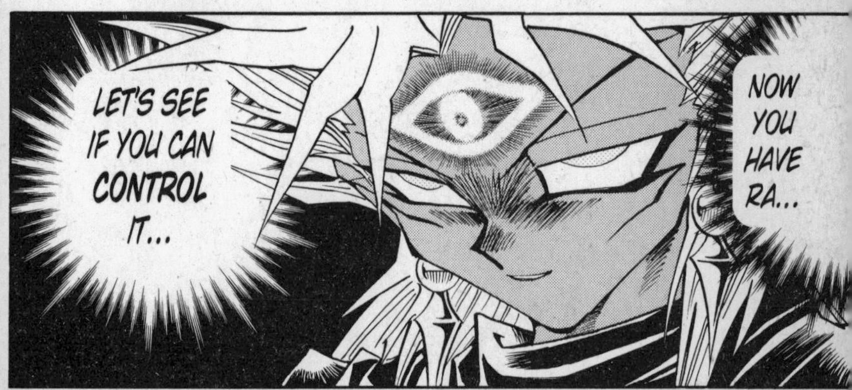
NOW YOU HAVE RA...
LET'S SEE IF YOU CAN CONTROL IT...

Duel 162: Descent of the God!

GI
GI
GI
GI
GOD HAS SWITCHED SIDES...
DUEL DISK

ZOOM

VWM
-AM

DID YOU SEE THAT?! MAI KUJAKU STOLE HIS GOD CARD!
...
EITHER ONE OF THEM CAN WIN NOW!
MARIK SAID, ONLY THOSE CONNECTED TO MILLENNIUM ITEMS CAN CONTROL GOD CARDS...

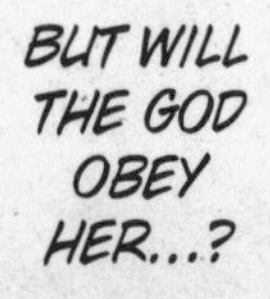
I DON'T REALLY BELIEVE THAT...
BUT WILL THE GOD OBEY HER...?

MAI KUJAKU
Life Points 2600

MARIK
Life Points 4000

GWOOO

MY TURN!!
FWP

A GOD CARD REQUIRES THREE SACRIFICES...!
THERE ARE TWO MONSTERS ON MARIK'S FIELD...
ZM ZM
I DON'T HAVE ANYTHING ON MY FIELD...
VISER DES
Attack 500
Invincible for two more turns
MAKYURA THE DESTRUCTOR
Attack 1900
ZM

I HAVE TO EVADE HIS ATTACKS...

UNTIL I CAN GET THREE MONSTERS ON THE FIELD!

WELL THEN...

LET'S SEE WHAT YOU CAN DO...

G' G' G'

AMAZONESS FIGHTER!!

AMAZONESS FIGHTER ★★★★
ATK/1500 DEF/1300

ATTACK MODE!

YES, YES...

JUST TRY AND ATTACK ME!

I'VE GOT A TRAP WAITING FOR YOU!

TURN END!

FWAM
I PLAY A FACE-DOWN CARD!
A FACE-DOWN CARD...!
AND I'LL ATTACK AMAZONESS FIGHTER WITH MAKYURA THE DESTRUCTOR!
EXECUTION BY KNIVES!
AMAZONESS FIGHTER Attack 1500
MAKYURA THE DESTRUCTOR Attack 1900
HE FELL FOR IT!!

FACE-DOWN SPELL CARD, ACTIVATE!
AMAZONESS SPELLCASTER
[SPELL CARD]
Until the end of this turn, switch the original ATK of a face-up monster on your side of the field with the original ATK of a face-up monster on your opponent's side of the field.
AMAZONESS SPELL-CASTER!!
D
G-
M
THANKS TO THIS MAGIC, OUR MONSTERS WILL SWITCH ATTACK POINTS!
MAKYURA THE DESTRUCTOR
Attack 1500
AMAZONESS FIGHTER
Attack 1900

AMAZONESS INSTANT KILL DANCE!
MAKYURA GOES DOWN!
...!
MARIK
Life Points 3600

TRAP CARD, REVEAL!

CARD OF LAST WILL!

MAKYURA IS DEAD, SO IN HIS HONOR, I'LL DRAW FIVE CARDS!

!!

HE'S GOING TO REPLENISH HIS HAND...!

CARD OF LAST WILL [TRAP CARD]

Activates when one of your monsters is defeated in combat. Draw cards until your hand has 5 cards.

ONE MORE THING...

MAKYURA'S SPECIAL POWER...
MAKYURA THE DESTRUCTOR
★★★★
During the turn this card is sent to the Graveyard, the owner of this card can activate Trap Card(s) from his/her hand.
ATK/1600 DEF/1200
ZM ZM ZM
#$@%...!
I DESTROYED IT THINKING HE DIDN'T HAVE A HAND...
KEH...
TASTE PAIN...
WHEN MAKYURA IS DESTROYED... I CAN PLAY A TRAP CARD FROM MY HAND!
TRAP CARD, ACTIVATE!!
NIGHTMARE WHEEL!
NIGHTMARE WHEEL
[PERMANENT TRAP CARD]
Select 1 monster. As long as this card remains face-up on the field, the selected monster cannot attack or change its battle position. This card inflicts 500 points of Direct Damage to your opponent's Life Points during each of your Standby Phases.
!!

READ THIS WAY
THOOOM
KEH KEH KEH...THE WHEEL WILL STRIP AWAY 500 OF YOUR LIFE POINTS EVERY TURN...
ALONG WITH INTENSE PAIN...
KREEK
NOW I'LL TORTURE YOUR AMAZON TO DEATH!
KREEK
KREEK
KREEK
KREEK
MAI!
...
THANKS...FOR TRYING TO TRAP ME...
HEH...

I'LL JUST PLAY THIS CARD!

DRAMATIC RESCUE
[TRAP CARD]

Activates when your monster falls for a trap. Return the targeted Monster Card to its owner's hand and Special Summon another monster from your hand in face-up Attack or Defense Position.

DRAMATIC RESCUE!

...

YOU'RE QUITE CLEVER...
BUT... THERE IS A WAY!
A WAY FOR ME TO SUMMON RA ON MY NEXT TURN...!
OH YES...?
...!?
HOW'S SHE GONNA GET THREE MONSTERS...?
I'LL SHOW YOU...
FIRST, I RESCUE THE AMAZONESS FIGHTER AND SEND HER BACK TO MY HAND!
LE
AP
HYO
OO
AND NOW...
I'LL PLAY THIS MONSTER CARD FROM MY HAND!
FWP

HARPY LADY ★★★★★
ATK/1300 DEF/1400
HARPY LADY!!
D-D-D-D-D
THE COMBO MAI IS GOING AFTER...!
I SEE!
THIS IS IT!
MAI'S BEST TRICK!!
THE AMAZONESS IS A GOOD GROUND FIGHTER, BUT SHE WAS JUST A DECOY.
WHAT I REALLY WANTED WAS MY GOOD OLD HARPY. AFTER ALL, SHE CAN FLY...
AND THAT'S NOT ALL!
NOW WATCH WHAT I'M GOING TO DO!

SPELL CARD... KALEIDO-SCOPE!
KALEIDOSCOPE
[SPELL CARD]
A monster equipped with this card turns into three duplicates of itself.
WITH THIS, I SPLIT MY HARPY LADY INTO THREE EQUALLY LOVELY MIRROR IMAGES!
I FORGOT ABOUT THAT!
WAY TO GO, MAI!!
G-
G-
G-
IN MY MAIN PHASE, I SACRIFICE THREE HARPIES...
AND SUMMON RA!!
G
G

DESCEND TO EARTH, SUN DRAGON RA!
FSH
G
THE SUN DRAGON RA
???
ATK/??? DEF/???
G
G
G
KEH KEH KEH...
DID YOU THINK YOU, OF ALL PEOPLE, COULD CONTROL GOD...?
G
YOU DON'T REALIZE...
THAT THE GOD ALREADY CONTROLS YOU...
G
WH-WHAT THE...?!
G
!!

ZWWMMM
IS THIS... THE SUN DRAGON RA?!
KHA HA HA...
WHAT'S GOING ON?!

DUEL DISK
DUEL 163: THE RISE OF RA!

ZM
TH-THIS IS WHAT RA LOOKS LIKE?!
IT'S LIKE A SPHERE OF GLOWING METAL...!
CAN THIS BE RA?!
ZM
KHA HA HA...
ZM
I GET THAT IT'S ROUND LIKE THE SUN...
BUT IS THAT **ALL?**
I **FEEL** ITS OVERWHELMING PRESENCE! AND IT **SHINES** WITH A **DIVINE LIGHT!**
BUT...I **FEEL** IT!!
ZM
ZM
THE THREE HARPY LADIES I SACRIFICED SHOULD HAVE MET THE SUMMONING CONDITIONS...
SO...HOW DID THIS HAPPEN?!

KHA HA HA HA HA...

RELAX, MAI KUJAKU...

WHAT YOU SUMMONED...

IS THE REAL THING...THE TRUE RA!

...!

THE SUN GOD RA...

THAT'S ITS TRUE FORM...?

...!

WH- WHAT THE...?!

G G G G G

2500

THE SUN DRAGON RA

IN THE TEXT SPACE OF THE CARD...SOME KIND OF HIERO- GLYPHS!?

SOMETHING'S NOT RIGHT...!
WHEN I TOOK THE GOD CARD FROM MARIK...
THE SUN DRAGON RA
???
ATK/??? DEF/???
THERE WAS NOTHING WRITTEN IN THE TEXT SPACE...
BUT...

NOW THERE'S DEFINITELY HIEROGLYPHS!
THE SUN DRAGON RA

KEH KEH KEH...WELL? CAN YOU DECIPHER THE SCRIPT?
IT CONTAINS THE *KEY* TO AWAKENING THE TRUE POWERS OF RA...

RA'S TRUE POWERS...!

THAT'S RIGHT...
THE TREMENDOUS POWERS OF GOD!

DARN! I WISH I COULD SEE IT!

WHAT'S IT LOOK LIKE?

WHAT SECRETS LIE IN THE TEXT OF THAT GOD CARD?

MOKUBA, ACTIVATE THE SATELLITE. USE THE ORBITAL CAMERA TO ZOOM IN ON MAI'S DUEL DISK.

OKAY, KAIBA!

GOOD IDEA!

G G G

IT'S NO USE...

THERE'S NO WAY I CAN TRANSLATE THIS...

IT'S IMPOSSIBLE, YOU CAN'T COMMAND GOD UNLESS YOU CAN READ THAT TEXT...
RA'S SPECIAL POWERS ARE FORBIDDEN TO YOU AS WELL...
BUT I'LL TELL YOU ONE THING...

THOSE LETTERS ARE...
HIERATIC TEXT!

HIERATIC TEXT...?!

WHAT THE HECK'S THAT?!

...!

IT WAS THE LANGUAGE USED FOR LAW, LITERATURE AND RELIGION IN ANCIENT EGYPT. UNLIKE THE COMMON DEMOTIC TEXT, ONLY THOSE OF SPECIAL STATUS WERE TAUGHT IT...
OF COURSE...
THE CHOSEN ONES CAN READ THE TEXT WITH THEIR HEARTS...
AND WE TOMB GUARDIANS KNOW IT AS WELL...

GIVE ME A BREAK...
THIS IS A CARD GAME! A CARD THAT ONLY SPECIAL PEOPLE CAN USE...?!

EVEN MAXIMILLION J. PEGASUS, THE CREATOR OF **DUEL MONSTERS**...

COULDN'T DECODE THE HIDDEN POWERS OF RA...

HE WAS FORCED TO LITERALLY TRANSCRIBE THE TEXT WRITTEN ON THE STONES...

I JUST CAN'T READ IT...

BUT THIS CARD HAS A SPECIAL FEATURE...

LIKE DISAPPEARING INK, THE LETTERS ONLY BECOME VISIBLE IN THE LIGHT EMITTED BY RA!

...

HE LET ME STEAL HIS CARD... KNOWING I CAN'T USE IT!

BA BAM

G G G

NOW--RA IS IN SPHERE MODE!

SOLVE THE MYSTERY AND CHANGE IT INTO BATTLE MODE!

KHA HA HA HA HA!

NOW, MAI KUJAKU! IT'S YOUR TURN!

...!!

D... D...

MAI KUJAKU
Life Points 2600

MARIK
Life Points 3600

RRGH...

BA

BAM

MAI!

THAT JERK MARIK! HE WAS NEVER AFRAID OF LOSING RA!

MARIK WANTED MAI TO SUMMON RA...!

MAI KUJAKU SACRIFICED THREE HARPY LADIES TO SUMMON THE SUN GOD...

RA'S ATTACK AND DEFENSE POINTS ARE DETERMINED BY THE TOTAL POINTS OF THE SACRIFICES...

HARPY LADY ★★★★★

ATK/1300 DEF/1400

IN OTHER WORDS, RA SHOULD HAVE 3900 ATTACK AND 4200 DEFENSE...

AND YET... THE GOD IS SILENT...

WHAT DOES THE TEXT SAY?! WHAT IS THE CONDITION TO ACTIVATE RA?!

IT'S NOT SHOWING ANY SIGNS OF ATTACKING OR DEFENDING...

ZM ZM ZM

GH...

I HAVE THE CARD...

BUT I CAN'T USE IT...!

UNLESS YOU DISCOVER THE SECRET OF GOD, YOU WILL FACE THAT HELLISH PAIN ONCE AGAIN...

I KNOW...

WHY DON'T YOU *PRAY?*

KEH KEH KEH...

I HAVE NO CHOICE...

BANG☆

I PLAY A FACE-DOWN CARD!

TURN END!

I JUST SET A TRAP... MIRROR WALL!

MIRROR WALL [PERMANENT TRAP CARD]
Halve the ATK of all your opponent's attacking monsters.

EVEN IF I CAN'T USE THE GOD CARD, AT LEAST HE WON'T BE ABLE TO ATTACK ME...!

MY TURN...

G
G
G
I SUMMON VISER SHOCK!

VISER SHOCK

★★★★

When this card is played on the field, all Reverse Cards on the field are returned to the respective players' hands.

ATK/800 DEF/800

G
G

TOO BAD...

THIS CARD WILL PUT AN END TO YOUR FACE-DOWN CARD...

NO...!

SHOOM

VISER SHOCK!
AND...
VISER DES!
DIRECT ATTACK ON THE PLAYER!
KLANG
KLANG
!!
KLANG
....!!
YAA-GGH!!!

GZZT
ZZT
ZZT
BEGIN THE EXECU- TION!!
ZZZ
ZZZT
AGG- GHH...
ZZT
ZZT
MAI KUJAKU Life Points 1300
MAI!!
SHE'S CAUGHT BY THOSE TWO TORTURE MONSTERS...!
THERE'S GOTTA BE A WAY FOR HER TO GET OUT!
MAI!!

KHA HA HA HA HA!
GIVE YOURSELF TO THE PAIN!
CURSE YOU... MARIK!
GRRR
KHA HA HA HA!
GYAAA!!!
QUITE A SHOW, ISN'T IT, YUGI?
WALKING ON THE EDGE OF DEATH...
FOR THIS WOMAN, *PAIN* IS HER ONLY PROOF THAT SHE STILL LIVES!
AND NOW...
I WILL BEGIN THE PREPARATIONS FOR THE SHADOW SACRIFICE...
THE SHADOW GAME...
SO MARIK'S PLANNING TO...!
YUGI... DID YOU KNOW...
THAT RA HAS *THREE* SPECIAL POWERS?
I'LL REVEAL JUST *ONE* OF THEM...
!!

WHAT?! THREE SPECIAL POWERS?!
VWAM
WHAT ...!?
HE'S CHANTING SOME KIND OF SPELL...! IS THAT ANCIENT EGYPTIAN...?!
G G G
G G G

G
THE SPHERE'S CHANGING SHAPE...
G
TH-THIS MUST BE...
G
THIS IS ONE OF RA'S SPECIAL POWERS...
G
G
G
G
G
GOD HIMSELF WILL SERVE THE PLAYER WHO UTTERS THE SACRED TEXT!

D-D-D
D-D!
THIS IS THE SUN DRAGON RA!

THE SUN DRAGON RA...!
ON MY TURN... WHEN RA ATTACKS...
I WILL INCINERATE THIS WOMAN IN A BLAZE OF FIRE...KHA HA HA HA!
AAGGHH...!
MAI!!

G
G
Duel 164: The Depths of Darkness!
G
KLANG★
G
KLANG★
G
RA...
...!
G
G
G
THE SPHERE'S OPENING UP AS HE CHANTS...!
!!

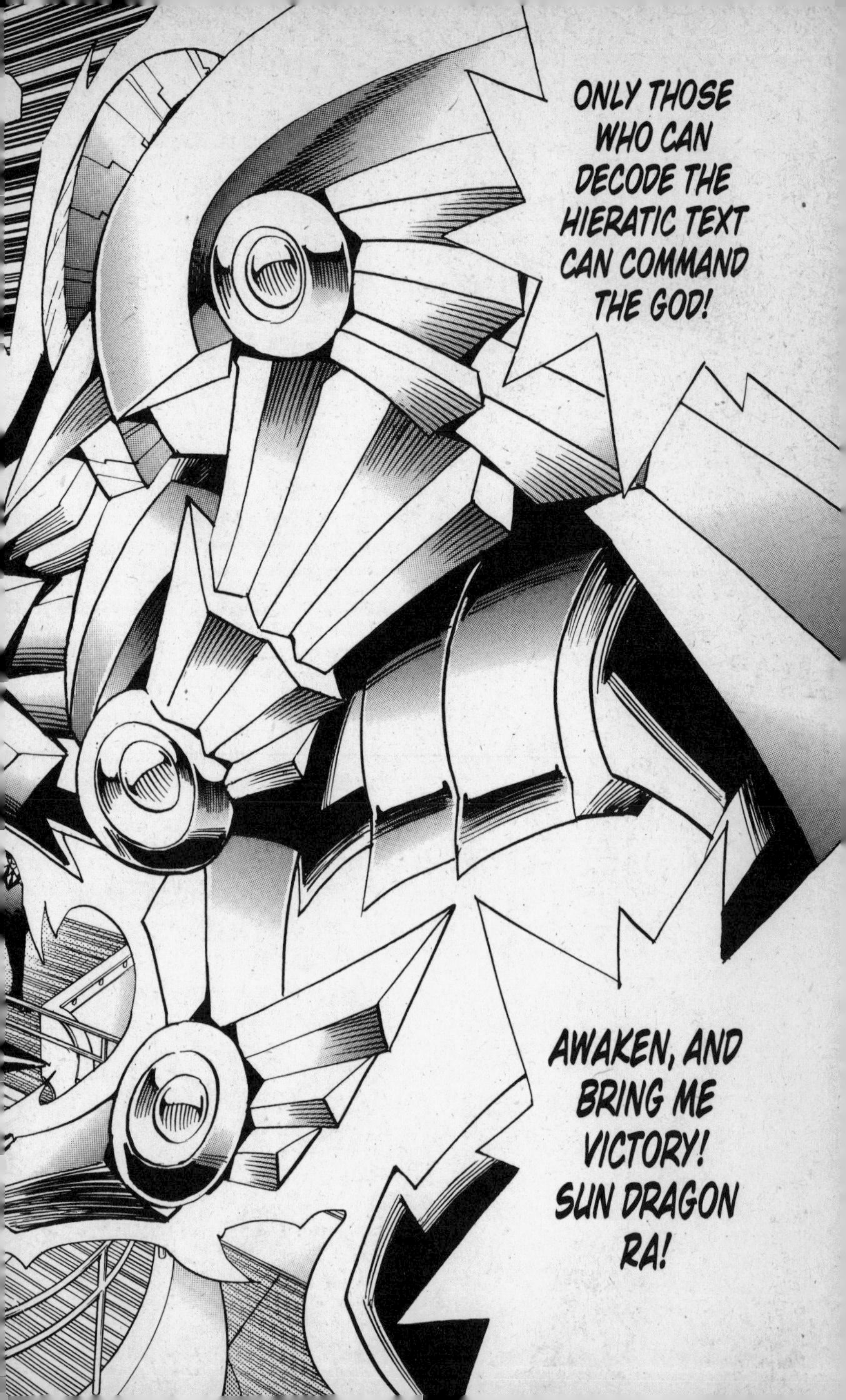
ONLY THOSE WHO CAN DECODE THE HIERATIC TEXT CAN COMMAND THE GOD!
AWAKEN, AND BRING ME VICTORY! SUN DRAGON RA!

DUEL 164: THE DEPTHS OF DARKNESS!
Z-D-D-D-R
THE SUN DRAGON RA
Attack 3900
Defense 4200

MAI!!
ON MARIK'S TURN, HE'LL ATTACK...AND MAI WILL TAKE 3900 DAMAGE!
BA
BA
IF THIS IS A SHADOW GAME...SHE'LL REALLY DIE!
BA
NGH...
BAM
KEH KEH KEH...YOU'RE A PERFECT SACRIFICE, MAI KUJAKU...
TIED TO THE TORTURE WHEEL...UNABLE TO MOVE YOUR ARMS AND LEGS...YOU CAN'T EVEN PLACE YOUR HAND ON YOUR DECK TO SURRENDER...
I'LL MAKE IT QUICK. JUST ONE SHOT FROM RA...
>HUFF<

BECOME ASH AND SPREAD INTO DARKNESS... MAI KUJAKU...

AGH! NO!

IF HE DOESN'T STOP, MAI'S DEAD!

STOP IT, MARIK!

THE DUEL IS OVER! YOU WIN! THERE'S NO NEED TO KEEP GOING!

...

KEEP YOUR EYES OPEN, YUGI...

I WILL SACRIFICE THE WOMAN TO THE SHADOWS...

AND DRAW OUT ALL OF YOUR HATRED...

MARIK, YOU SCUM...!

ON MY BACK IS CARVED THE **SEAL OF MEMORIES...**

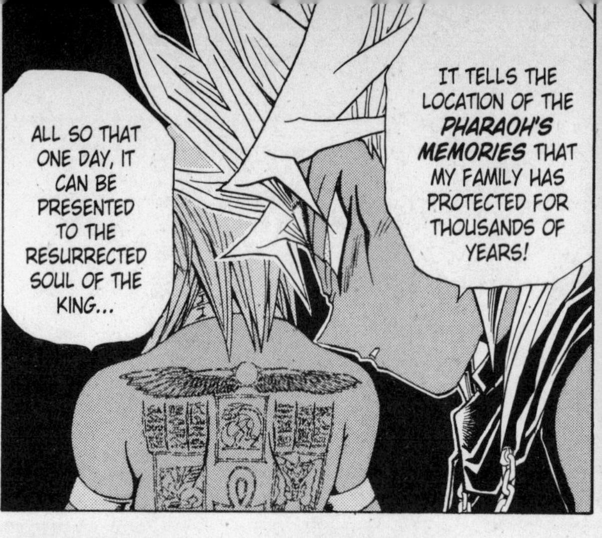
IT TELLS THE LOCATION OF THE ***PHARAOH'S MEMORIES*** THAT MY FAMILY HAS PROTECTED FOR THOUSANDS OF YEARS!
ALL SO THAT ONE DAY, IT CAN BE PRESENTED TO THE RESURRECTED SOUL OF THE KING...

THE SEAL OF MEMORIES!

FOR THAT PURPOSE AND THAT PURPOSE ONLY, COUNTLESS GENERATIONS OF MY ANCESTORS LIVED AND DIED...
OUR ONLY BIRTHRIGHT WAS DARKNESS... THE DEPTHS OF DARKNESS... AND A DEEP SCAR...
DESPAIR AND PAIN...
THAT IS ALL...

...
PFT...
KHA HA HA...

KHA HAA HA HAA HA HA!
DO YOU LIKE IT? THAT IS THE TRAUMA THAT DOMINATES MY OTHER SELF!
DARKNESS ROBBED HIM OF HIS FREEDOM... AND EVEN MORE DARKNESS WAS BORN IN HIS SELF-PITYING HEART!

THE *PAIN* AND *HATRED* THAT EXISTS WITHIN HIS DARK HEART...

THESE THINGS BELONG TO *ME*...

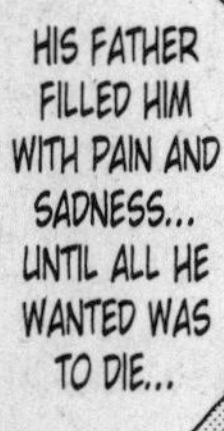

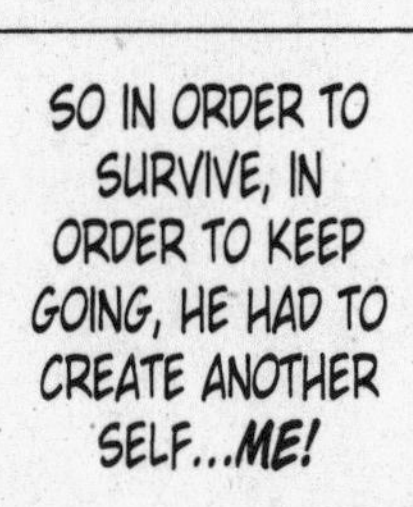

BUT THERE WAS ONE THING WHICH STOOD IN MY WAY...
I CAN ONLY COME OUT WHEN HE IS FILLED WITH RAGE...

BUT THAT MAN RISHID...
HE CALMED MARIK'S ANGER...AND WITHOUT EVEN KNOWING, HE SEALED ME AWAY WITH THE CARVING ON HIS FACE...

I WAS CONFINED DEEP INSIDE MARIK'S HEART...

KEH KEH KEH...BUT NOW THAT RISHID IS GONE...
I AM FINALLY THE RULER OF THIS BODY!

WHAT DO I WANT...?
KEH KEH...
I HAVE NO NEEDS.
BUT...
IF YOU REALLY WANT AN ANSWER...

WHAT DO YOU WANT?!
DO YOU WANT THE GOD CARDS?
OR..

I WANT TO DESTROY...
ALL LIGHT... ALL ORDER...
AND ALL LIFE BESIDES MY OWN!
B-BMP
I WANT TO DESTROY EVERYTHING!
DESTRUCTION IS MY ONLY PLEASURE!
DESTRUCTION GIVES BIRTH TO MY WORLD!
THE DARK WORLD!
ZM
MARIK...
ZM ZM ZM
RRG...
BEFORE MARIK CAN ATTACK...
I'LL GET MAI OUT OF THERE!
DASH

AND NOW...
I WILL SACRIFICE THIS MISERABLE WOMAN...
TM TM TM
HEY! LOWER THE DUEL STAGE!
GRAB
!!
NO WAY!
WE CAN'T LET A THIRD PARTY INTERFERE WITH A DUEL!
@#$%!
GET OUTTA MY WAY!
YOU'LL BE DISQUALIFIED, JONOUCHI!!
IS THIS THE SWITCH?!
MAI!!

READ THIS WAY
JONO-UCHI...
IT'S OVER FOR ME...
IT'S MY TURN...
RA! BURN THAT WOMAN!!
MAI!!

GRR RR
SUN DRAGON RA! ATTACK!
THE SUN DRAGON RA
Attack
3900

IF THAT HITS MAI, SHE'LL...
MAI!
DIE.
GOD BLAZE CANNON!!
MAI KUJAKU
Life Points 1300

G
G
MAI!!
G
GET OUTTA HERE!
...!
JONO-UCHI...
G
OH MY GOSH! HE'S...!
G
KATS-UYA!
SPIRI
WHAT ARE YOU DOING!
MOVE! YOU'LL GET HIT!
G
SHUT UP...
I CAN'T JUST WATCH MY FRIEND GET KILLED!

I STILL HAVE LIFE POINTS LEFT...
I CAN'T TURN MY BACK ON AN OPPONENT...
ARE YOU CRAZY?! HURRY UP AND GET OUTTA HERE!
IT'S NO USE...
I CAN'T MOVE...
THIS CAN'T BE...!
I KNOW THIS TORTURE THING ISN'T REAL...IT'S LIKE VIRTUAL REALITY...BUT MAI'S BODY WON'T BUDGE!
G
IS THIS MARIK'S SHADOW GAME?!
G
G
ULP...!
G
G
...
YOU NEED TO GET OUT OF HERE, JONOUCHI!
YOU STILL HAVE A DUEL TO FIGHT!

JONO...
G
I DON'T CARE!
JONO-UCHI...
YOU CAME BACK TO GET ME...JUST LIKE THE LAST TIME...
IT MADE ME HAPPY...
G
THAT YOU CALLED ME A FRIEND...
DON'T THROW YOUR LIFE AWAY! RUN!
THANKS...
G
G
MAI...
THE REASON I ENTERED THIS TOURNAMENT... WAS SO I COULD FIGHT YOU ONCE AGAIN...
THAT'S THE ONLY WAY I KNOW...TO LET YOU KNOW HOW I FEEL...
G
G

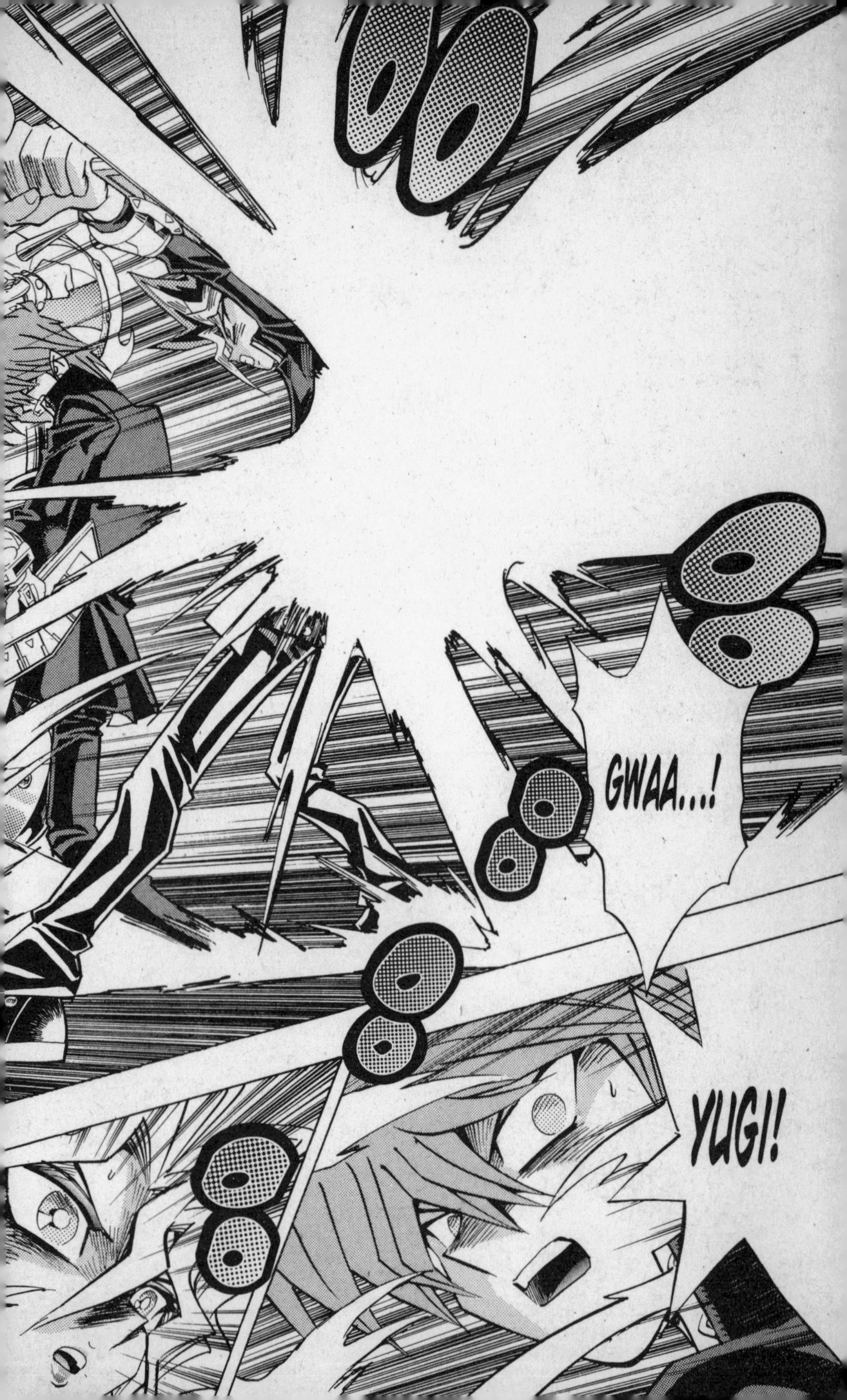
GWAA...!
YUGI!

TO BE CONTINUED IN *YU-GI-OH!: DUELIST* VOL. 19!

MASTER OF THE CARDS

The "Duel Monsters" card game first appeared in volume two of the original **Yu-Gi-Oh!** graphic novel series, but it's in **Yu-Gi-Oh!: Duelist** (originally printed in Japan as volumes 8-31 of **Yu-Gi-Oh!**) that it gets really important. As many fans know, some of the card names are different between the English and Japanese versions. In case you play the game, or you're interested in playing, here's a rundown of some of the cards in this graphic novel. Some cards only appear in the **Yu-Gi-Oh!** video games, not in the actual trading card game.

FIRST APPEARANCE IN THIS VOLUME	JAPANESE CARD NAME	ENGLISH CARD NAME
p.7	*Ôke no Shinden* (Temple of the Kings)	Royal Temple
p.7	*Selket no Monshô* (Crest of Selket)	Seal of Selket (NOTE: Not a real game card)
p.7	*Seijû Selket* (Holy Beast/Beast God Selket)	Mystical Beast of Selket (NOTE: Not a real game card)
p.8	*Fûkon no Seihai* (Chalice of Sealed/Bound Soul)	Cup of Sealed Soul (NOTE: Not a real game card)
p.8	*Baby Dragon*	Baby Dragon
p.9	*Madô Kishi Giltia* (Magic Conducting/Guiding Knight Giltia)	Giltia the D. Knight
p.9	*Yûgô* (Fusion)	Polymerization

FIRST APPEARANCE IN THIS VOLUME	JAPANESE CARD NAME	ENGLISH CARD NAME
p.20	*Ra no Yokushinryû* (Ra the Winged God Dragon) (NOTE: The kanji for "sun god" is written beside the kanji for "Ra.")	The Sun Dragon Ra (NOTE: Called "The Winged Dragon of Ra" in the English anime and card game)
p.94	*Amazoness no Kenshi* (Amazoness Swordswoman)	Amazoness Swords Woman
p.97	*Shokeinin—Makyura* (Executioner—Makyura)	Makyura the Destructor
p.99	*Amazoness no Dokyûtai* (Amazoness Longbow Archery Corps)	Amazoness Archers
p.103	*Inochi no Tsuna* (Rope of Life)	Rope of Life
p.112	Amazoness Chain Master	*Amazoness no Kusaritsukai* (Amazoness Chain User)
p.116	*Manrikimajin Viser Death* (Vise Devil/Demon God/ Genie Viser Death)	Viser Des (NOTE: Not a real game card)
p.122	*Maisô no Ude* (Arm of Burial)	Grave Arm (NOTE: Not a real game card)

FIRST APPEARANCE IN THIS VOLUME	JAPANESE CARD NAME	ENGLISH CARD NAME
p.132	*Amazoness no Jusoshi* (Amazoness Curse Master)	Amazoness Spellcaster
p.132	*Kyûshutsugeki* (Dramatic Rescue)	Dramatic Rescue
p.133	*Amazoness no Kakutôsenshi* (Amazoness Hand-to-Hand Fighter)	Amazoness Fighter
p.134	*Yuigon no Fuda* (Card of Last Will)	Card of Last Will (NOTE: Not a real game card)
p.138	*Gômonsharin* (Torture/Rack Wheel)	Nightmare Wheel
p.142	*Harpie Lady*	Harpy Lady
p.143	*Mangekyô: Karei naru Bunshin* (Kaleidoscope: Splendid Doppelganger)	Kaleidoscope (NOTE: Called "Elegant Egotist" in the English anime and card game)
p.157	*Ginmaku no Mirror Wall* (Mirror Wall of the Silver Screen)	Mirror Wall
p.158	*Cyber Shock*	Cyber Shock (NOTE: Not a real game card)

IN THE NEXT VOLUME...

Yugi and Jonouchi risk their lives to save Mai from Marik's bloodthirst...but will it be enough? Then, Kaiba faces the mysterious eighth duelist, an Egyptian woman with the power to see the future. Kaiba's only hope for victory may lie in the sands of time, in the secrets engraved long ago in an ancient stone slab! Plus the horrifying secret origin of Marik!

COMING FEBRUARY 2007!

SHONEN JUMP manga!

Our survey is now available online.
Go to: ***www.SHONENJUMP.com/mangasurvey***